The Shape of a Forest

Jemma L King

Jemma L King currently teaches literature and creative writing at Aberystwyth University where she also completed her doctoral thesis. She won the The Terry Hetherington Young Writer of the Year Award in 2011 and her creative and academic work has been published internationally. She is a founding member of the Centre for Women, Writing and Literary Culture and is a reviewer of contemporary literature for numerous publications.

The Shape of a Forest

Jemma L King

Parthian
The Old Surgery
Napier Street
Cardigan
SA43 1ED

www.parthianbooks.com

First published in 2013
© Jemma L King 2012
All Rights Reserved

ISBN 9781-908069894

Editor: Kathryn Gray
Cover by www.theundercard.co.uk
Typeset by Elaine Sharples
Printed and bound by Dinefwr Press, Llandybie,
Wales

Published with the financial support of the Welsh
Books Council.

For my parents

Contents

Amelia Earhart

In 2010, a team of researchers from The International Group for Historic Aircraft Recovery discovered the remains of a 1930s female American castaway on the remote and uninhabited island of Nikumaroro in the middle of the Pacific Ocean. It is strongly believed that the castaway was Amelia Earhart, the pioneering female pilot who disappeared in 1937 whilst attempting to circumnavigate the world by air.

i

For someone so accustomed to speed,
silence and stillness was something.
It fell to a hum.
It widened.

First, an inventory of quiet invaded and took root.
Each variety lived
and sang one note.

But this shelf fell off, deeply,
plaintively cut to the igneous core.
The air plucked at bird string,
marsupial chatter, and
tapped irregular fingers to it.

Each scrambled song an insult
to one who craved an engine and a wing.

At first, she went mad.

ii

The damning thing was
the finger bone. Hers, they said.

That and the pre-war American cosmetics. Misplaced
in a land without a metal press or edges,
nature powdered to a pigment,
or hands to press the buttons.

That, and the upturned oyster shells,
shallow buckets laid out in rows
to plug up the sand,
drain the sky, resist
the wretched equatorial
heat.

The desperation that brands the spot
where the star imploded
in the most sparse
edge of the galaxy. Unnoticed

surrounded by star birds and star crabs
caught in the gravity
of their own orbits.

iii

The crabs ate her,
crushing the bones that
once hung bravery,
eyes that held the earth's curve,

the heart that burst adrenaline
drilled it to the tips of grasping fingers
feeling life, even in the face of the spiked sea.
Electra's crunch and spasm groaning.
The sea church settles
and takes pity.

iv

Amelia fell upwards and
was laid like a pearl on the shoreline.

v

I imagine her whole and tanned,
her clothing dirtied but intact.
Her right hand loosely on her hip,
the other shielding squinting eyes
from sun which levels her up.

She looks out before looking in
to the mountain tip of her new island,
the horizon as empty as the stomach.
Birthdays pass, Christmases pass.
The slow collapse
into new years.

She's stood there, blinking.

Water Music

The stream is coughing notes
up on the rocks,
frothing them out
and hissing

trails of bubbles,
a troop of dancers;
racing stone edges towards the
width and drop ahead.

Full rain
pitches her lungs,
splits them on flint islands,
bursts on the gravity
of the fall's edge.
Unbound by physics,
she collapses into
white myth.

Down the river, a quieter affair,
dull percussive chords.
Irregular salmon vault and
side slap
the calm on descent,

clawed back
by the estuary
in aubade, singing
to her sons of the sea,
calling them home.

Nuclear

Here all of us are
crackling anxious
to love.

But there is an alchemist
wanting for myth
to buy his way in,
with his strangler's
verve and bargain.

The air is tattooed
with a pulse.
Something lives
beyond the body.
A shattered blissbox.
The thighs'
wax and wane
remembered.

The white windowed
filament of time
is burning.

Winter for the Robin

The night had broken down in inches,
marked by raised choirs of bird noise.

The robin was face down when I found him.
His wings, glacial triangles,
mocked his form,
strapped him down
to the newly found grip
of the pond.

Now, the snow-packed mountains with baby faces
still on, loosen their robes
shaking out survivors of stiffened sleep.
Later, the canvas of snow
unpeels from the hills,
shows the grass
stalks fighting a tightened
earth
to get loose.
Air has wrung out each stray atom;
it is a naked face of glass.

Unknowing, there is a fight
at the bird table.
Fattened thrushes, winter broken.
They are not mourning the missing friend.
The hardness of the hardest of seasons
is designed to kill.
That is what the winter is for,
to divide last year's from this.

One robin
is broken and cloven
from the red,
and startled to sleep in white sheets.

The Beginning

My conception was a blur to me.
The first I knew was the
warm hand over the smutch
of me.

For a month I lay yellowed
in her fabric, adulterating and eating.

What was my shape? I couldn't tell.

I grew –
stretching my fingers
skywards, corrupting the
backbone, my jaws
at the womb.

The doctor said I had potential,
tried to scissor me free
from my mother.

That sky opened right up.
A shrieking red blade
was cursing me in waves.

I divided, divided
over-expressing myself, apparently.
A bloom of atoms
ranged from the blood.
I hid inside
the bones and shivered.

They sent sticky sinews,
arrested my
many faces, blinded me,
froze

the chromosomes
that made me.

Japan

i

From the classroom, the first
shriek of Japan's black lacquer
cracking.
From the street, the head funk
of raining brick and concrete,
the red flair of towns.
From the cities, a mouth not quite deep enough
to swallow the dead
in the collapse
of a country's scaffolding.
From the people: a love prayer
to tables, to save them.

The landmass falling
eight inches east.

ii

The water pulls flat, sharpens as
the gun shot rips across
stinging
a hem of metres,
standing
on hind legs.
The ocean screams
as black flesh swells
a rock wall,
bends a target.

The oiled waves are coming.
The oiled waves are coming.

iii

And now the cats in houses
and now the cows in fields
and now the children in schools.

And now

a mud flat, an estuary sweep.

iv

Now the air is flecking with
a microscopic hail, gelling fibres
to skin and cloth, finding routes in.

Making clay of organs,
making clay of this nation.

The Man

They made him big.
Strong enough to digest
a pen of thieves and criminals.

Thin air laced towards Samhain,

villagers worked briskly, spiral-painted faces
twitching with the effort
of twining man from branch and stick.

The Druid came to bless it
as Taranis banged the floor,
sending mountains reeling,
sheep scattering like sand on a drum.

The storm God shook his sun-cross, sent his eight
spokes of intellect crashing skies above the Gauls to
   the Danube.
The stars burst with electroshock
and swollen cracking.

Pitchforks and pulleys metalled his birth.
He stood sharpening the hill point
with clayed face, outstretched arms.

Men filled his veins,
advancing under whip slice
and promise.
The villagers, half drunk on gallow frenzy,
turned their palms and fists skywards for explanation.

The Druid's arm fell to this smoke prayer,
the timbre dry to the first pinch
of flame, the bloom of cinder
theory chancing heavenwards.

Taranis, pleased with this oven of God-love,
finger-stuffed the dead back into their graves,
defused his thunder stock.

On the Marriage of William Wales and Kate Middleton…

He's dead pleased,
but he's not a royalist, no;
he's Welsh for God's sake,
but he's pleased.

The plastic sacks are as stuffed
as bodies in a skin.
They lie twenty deep, fifteen
across, lazy

as a teenager, awaiting
final shape and form.
His fingers will limber it, give it pulse,
freeze it
in fire.

The coffee skin has
thickened in neglect
but his pen won't stop

drawing.

He sits back and studies
the loops of the W, the flourish of the K.
The bags are
waiting.

Bear handed, he splits the face
of a bag and hews a lump
of clay, slaps it

on the table.

Translates it into money.

Genghis

In some sweaty shade of gold
the horse protracts
his nostrils.
Constellations of muscles
flick one by one,
stormed waves of
sharp sable.

On this equine tank
is a man of blood.
His women are split like fruit,
spored with armies.
His machine eats a map
stains it

with a double helix
and dead men.

Half the known world is his.
His empire is a fire.

His eyes open
on every village.
His little suckling mouths
are a million.

Hegarty

Your fur was lightly
smoking a glitter dust
in the dark.

Nothing could be extracted from this.
You were divided from me
by the filth of a shed window,
by the forces that had taxidermied you in the night.
Your radiant black was
a bag of death polluting the yellow tent
you slept on.

You were an unwanted thing, Hegarty.
The uncontested item of a marriage collapsed.
Prettiness had been ripped off your face
in an early fight. Now, at fifteen,
those one-eyed, brawling features
had no ink in the list
of contested things. So I took you.

You inspired fear in some who jumped
at your senile, loudmouthed devil bawl,
the over-eager advance to the lap.

*

This week
I threw your name
at the trees and rocks, but it
bounced back,
undeliverable.

I knew then,
as my feet went through the motions,
that the air had wrung itself clean
of you.

All week, my voice met
satellites
pointing the wrong way,
and I felt it.

But this early April shower had
bruised up the morning,
soaked the skin
of the earth in waves
between the sun's forced glare
firing up the slates like
churned-up silver.

In this,
the unlikeliest of things
became mirrors, lit the
damp corners and

there you were, behind the window.

There was the shell that wore you.
The feet you'd slipped on, dustily painting
car bonnets and tables, were now
the furniture of a dead person.

Ed dug the hole, placed you
into some layer with

careful handfuls of earth
that fell to a heavy fist.

Asanas

Here, below the 49th
octave, the world's story
made hieroglyph in red
cell and bone.

I am tracing the
outside curve
of muscle, a deathbed
of two dozen vermillion
petals.

A franchise of neurons
unlocked
and growing.
The crescent moon is
waxing full,

unhooks me
from Samsara.

The Belvedere Apollo

When Anzio coughed him up in 1489,
Apollo was dragging the bones of the sun
across Europe.
Here was the joke of prophecy –
those stone eyes
really had seen through
the fug of two thousand years.

They shelled the God from the pack that bore him,
set his legs standing
in Belvedere.
The quiet grandeur of his gaze,

confused.
His muscles the
tension of a long shot
contrapposto.

But the strophium
still banded his head. Relieved,
he settled
and slept.

The laurels would find new
worship amongst poets,
the artists would charge him,
stuff him with the heady bluff
of Adamic myth.
America would shoot him

to the stars.

Nigeria

In Landrovered shade,
the lion is gold against rust.
Muscled velvet belts blue
and swats a fly.
The boiled air melts space;
his face wrinkles.

The passenger seat holds a man picked dry.
The guns are still in the boot.

His boned hand continues the drive
into that tree. The fingers are just rocks now
and emptied.

But the hand belonging to
the fly-bitten brain once
followed command
and killed.

Machetes peeled the place
back. Drowned the choke
of life shinned
and limbless.

The lion's eyes blind
to this Ozymandias of bricks set in squares,
tyres hanging from trees.
A doll, a ball.

Walls

(i) The Girl

Pulling inwards the
elasticated wrists of the
puffa jacket,
she puts one foot flat
against the pebbledash
wall of the corner shop
that used to be a house.

She strains her ears against the assault of the rain,
listening for the whistle and groan
of the ancient Crosville bus.
The inside of her jacket
is a portable safe
stashing stolen
crisps and sweets.
She'll starve herself
fat on contraband
sugar.
She fingers her nylon pocket,
broken through and frayed.
The lighter has sunken
into the flesh
of the coat.

Where the crumbs and padding live.

(ii) The House

The windows are unwelcome.
Each pitted frame befriending the frost
allowing black damp
to scale and thrive.

There is nobody home.

Every wall is a threat
concealing what has happened,
boxing it up with Sellotape.
Some sorry attempt at
something home shaped.

It staggers, drunk
on its own weight,
wearing its layers of
paint as frayed mass.
The very word 'rape' a cluster bomb
of violence threatening to shatter
through her skin.

It wouldn't be worth it. She
takes up drink. Makes a friend of the mirror
that helps her craft her mask.
Lives between her bedroom and other worlds,
the future she is sure will come. Her ceiling
is the canvas of these dreams, marbled in
cigarette smoke, blurring into
cities and streets.

This house will kill her.

Hymn

I'd gently xylophone your ribs
with naked fingers,
should you license the closed-eye
smile of the
dawn.

Give me your 2am.
I'd pack it tight with five strings of
your voice. Wordless
and hot.

And the day will be
a winter's cold kiss of the tide,
tempering the myth
of us, and

that cloud of twisted whale spine

dissolving above

to dusk, and the death
of your thoughts
on the hinge
of our bodies.

The Kiss

I am beyond calibration.
About as together
as the meat of sea water
choking apart.

Why don't you call?

Every woman knows this story.
Each minute fracturing
into reminders
of you. Memory

courting me
in your absence.

These hands? Yours.
My capillaries filling
idiotically remembering
the smash of lips,
my hands reaching ribs and palming
skin. Us, the hot
scandal of the dance floor. The warmth
of you
against
me.

Curtains

He slinks, by instinct,
close to the ground.
His hip bones
meander a path to the mouse.

Only exposing himself
in a final leap across the Serengeti
of the backyard.
In his mind, he is a lion.

On his prey, he
posts pressure through the tip
of each claw. Each pinpoints
pain on hinges.
The first the mouse knows,
is the pang of being opened.

A furious fight.
Louder cries than the mouse
knew he could. The cat
bites at the stomach and skull.

The cat brain knows its aim.

He will stop the moving
from moving
because he can.

Mansion

Your front pillars have buckled.
The sun's veins
withdrawing,

dragging with them
the lines of a calendar,
the hands of a clock.

All is quiet and
the strain of silence
fights the weight

of granite.

Doors fall and seal rooms.
Create tombs out
of grandeur.

Vinegar splits stone –
it is not immortal,
and pales to atoms,

a plant again, a cockroach.

Found

His skinny limbs, cold
broken, took flight
through smoke-struck air.
The cat chewed laces held fast,
secured shoddy leather
to the frog-belly white
of his feet.

The mud-beaten ball
struck a side-on ankle,
cleared the jumper posts.
To his eyes, it was Wembley.

The ball scuffed
a shallow dirt valley
on some broken hinge.
It clasped only air,
pulling bookends of history
together.

The yellow metal grinned
toothlessly. Celtic knotted and
rubied,
its purpose
worked free of itself.

Why did it live here?

This field was a root-bed,
left clean of town planners,
council houses, shops.

His sense of balance
suddenly gummed and flexed
as trees replaced houses,
houses replaced trees.
His football pitch a palace.

Ogley Hay inside out.

Sun

I am

thinking how wintered
a June evening
can look.

Deceptive. Brass
embryo this morning –
now no one's idol.

An old god. Died
with its people
mid-worship.

Sex

Her thick strips of eyelashes
anchor the men compliant.
Her lips, a shelf of gloss.
Malleable, they will dog fight
each other for one night
with the girl.
Eyes search
the radius of the room,
for that one guy
for one night.
Later, the brain box
dissolves to chasm
and magic. She can't quite feel it,
but he rucks himself
into infancy.
She goes through the motions.
Empty
as cells divide.

Tomorrow,
they will be two people,
blood, spit and semen,
separate and leaving.

One year later,
no man in no room
wants to admit
that he was that one guy,
for one night,
that split her and
buried something inside.

But she is two again.

The Birth of Shaman's Daughter

Shaman stamped the ground,
feeling spaces between
body and soil.
March sun seared his eyes
already doloured sightless.
He ripped at the grass
each broken green neck,
a sacrifice.

He hoped.

And inside the earth, this tap, tap, tapping.
A creaking ghost clock
counting down and pinching
legs and sleepy toes.
The earth swelled.
Foined weight fell sideways, griping
noises nature had forgotten.

Elements rubbed her forehead and checked pulses.
The love damp air found
capillaries and filled them.

Here was a new door.

Her throat a barb of choke,
clearing.
Worm cold, those chewed-up, flued
muscles found each other, bit on
crude nerves
and lifted.
So forcefully,
that ground found her
from below.

Still amphibian limbs, sticky
and broken.
On her side, she reached naked
for the blur
breaking the sun.
His oak frame
a mast pinning earth to sky.

Something was trying
from her throat –
some half-baby mewl.
She saw him turn,
she heard the shriek.
She was alone.

She would have to learn to spell again.

Astronomy

As captive as the dark is,
anchored to the earth with pivotal force.
The sky a menagerie of squawking light.
I am trapped in all this space

nightly.

Armour

is a talisman tattoo
against the blade
that knows the eye's root.

I saw it with my own eyes, three tanks were blown up,
   three vehicles were blown up

It is an invisibility cloak
that protects the wearer
in this bone-scuffed vent
of Islam.

These are young children; 18, 19, 20 with arms and
   legs blown off. That is the reality

Skin suits of metal and canvas
hide the blood pumped tides of man,
saves from the ripcord of head caverns, exploding,
the suction of lungs expelled
through the mouth
under forces of Moab bombs

You didn't see where those bullets landed. You didn't see
   what happened when the mortar landed

in this crunk of stone and bloodfall.
Desert veins
are rivers of skin rippers,
fly-blown mouths.

Witnessed the arrival of four to five US helicopters –
  carrying between them 10-15 American casualties –
  each day

Brawny US tanks, each a small country
carrying walls
and men to the cause
to pick a path
on which to leave
an empty bed.

Ana

Under those Machu Picchu ribs,
the heart is still pumping out the
flux of life
against the ink
of her journal

choosing bones and escape.

Her lean blood braids its way
unwarranted, gasping at
the bloated
balloon of stomach
begging for bread.
Still the apparatus hurls itself forward,
pints per minute.
The mechanism as
taut as rag rugs.

She must cut it open to stop it, drain her life
like an ellipsis.
Grounds herself
in starless vaults, stopping.

In the barn

In the barn, and
my cigarette ash
floats like snow
on a current of
stale straw air
and tears.

A bomb of
sheep calling
shocks the system –
the silence,
never.

I'll sit here
ask the grass
for an answer.
They tell me
that even the dying
can make mountains
on the heart monitor.

En route to the airport

North-bound for Liverpool to Paris.
3am and

Runcorn's refineries, cut off, stage-left
of the dual carriageway, as though
my eyes are supposed to look away
out of politeness.

The landscape scowls in fluorescence,
expels
the night shift of
men emerging greased with
ticking, creeping illnesses
growing on their skins.

Not quite forgotten in Versaille.
The next day, my graduation
no foil for those

waning columns of smoke,
not touching,
abandoned to the sky.

St. Hilda's

She told me about her college,
an Oxbridge school of conversions
bought on cheap vodka,
curiosity.

The idea was intriguing.

Her own body
reflected in the gauze of the other's skin.
The dumb-speak of walls.

There, she
stepped outside of norms,
graduated activist,
evangelical of the
honest animal
fraction found in the dorm,
in the bar.

She found man-ling,
girl-things to play with.
Cute-things, boy-things,
same-thing.

The love shocked her like a fault line.

You

This lack of energy.
Irresponsible, the lack
of you. Short

of anything useful.
You're not here,
pointless trying to be.

I invent your embrace,
as you do in my want-
oness, my energy.

Geological

I have been igneous,
molten and now
solidified.

broken
           from the rock face,
bolted to the rock bed.

Winter

The way you live
in the shadows,
around rims of coffee cups.

Nobody forces me to
feel, but I love the sadness
of you.

I can't look at you today,
my empty vessel,
winter above the sand.

Koyaanisqatsi

Koyaanisqatsi (Hopi for 'Unbalanced Life') is a film by Godfrey Reggio made in 1982. The film consists primarily of slow motion and time-lapse footage of cities across the United States. The film contains neither dialogue nor a vocalised narration. It displays the effects of technology on the environment, and on people.

Spread before me,   complexity
        in pageant.

        Which way?

Nightmares clad me bedridden, hoaxed in fear soaked
  in sweat.

Nocturnal Arizona.
Like   the   stones   stand

        with bound hands.

The stars, taunting.

First week without you

Magnesium sunset stained the sea
but my shoes were studded to the asphalt strip.
Too spiky for beach terrain.

You would have loved
this sulphur sky,
the platoons of ice
terrorising the surface of the sea.

I can see your face at wonder,
your eyes crinkling in thrill.

The lack of camera.

I think on the
day you dropped me off,
and all the way down the hill, the hail
knifed at me in force.

I reported back to you, girlish
and charged with the elements.

But here, the sky
plays some
shaking concerto, unravelling

ionic webs,

and you are not here.

Butterfly

That summer was as sharp as the edge
of a butterfly wing.
Moments on the corkboards
of unwanted postcards and lists reminding me of what
  I have not done.
At that point
I didn't realise that there was a point
to savour. But it was netted and pinned

down regardless.

Prayer

And shaped like sex
but crawling
with power. I'll stalk
your streets.
My hip bone,
my hip bone
I'll beat you.
The disjointed split
of symmetrical
heat. I'll
attack you when
you are alone.

The Returning

It was funny, you know.
Witnessing my own death.
Beyond the door, decaying
piles of mess. Two months of
packets and papers and tins.
Ashtrays overflowing.
Upstairs the CDs last played,
awaiting a game partner.
The plug unplugged, frayed
wires. Long faces.
The damp.

Just two months.
They could've allowed me that.
Instead they mourned,
covered me over and
piled up the washing.
Life stopped when I stopped.
But it was funny, seeing what if.
I stood, and smoked and cried.
They didn't even realise
that the rest of me had gone,
but they knew that
the ashtrays needed emptying.

The Time

So far,
she had spun by uncaught.
She is devious

a bag of nothing
for your everything.

Her frosted eyes
are blind
to pleas, clumsy thumbs

and fingers. You
won't free it,
she'll boil

you down
to sepia and dust
still kicking.

The road is truncated.
An inflexible bracket.
And you, a thick black line.
An arrow that
points to bed.

December

June is a felled wood
bowing at the threshold
of ice-filled breath.

The degrees,
slipping through summer's
fingers. The trees,
X-rays of former selves.

Today brought this change.

My writer's reflex for
the fireside – looked up
from the shell of a conker,

the smell of a bonfire.
My balance is not in
the abundance of light, but

a chosen flicker and crackle.
December sky
was invented for Orion's

candles. His far-off
country, as cold
as the poles.

July

I live in July
as dust sits on a negative.

'God, it's so hot,
isn't it lovely?'

Yes, and bland.
A still life, and me,
the vase.

Misophonic

Abrasive mouth.
You are the spring in the bed
that sticks in the rib.
A noise rape
from the base of
evolution's chain.
The glass to cut
your throat could
never be deep enough.
Shut the clotted
gum of your speak!
The howl that sits in
my mouth,
swallowed
by your black hole
of teeth itching noise-
glottals that stick
and congeal in the
air. Hanging like
markers of territory.

Madame Coco

Owlheaded Minx-
was born with
eyes full of wisdom,
handfuls of glass.

Teeth you don't want to mess with.

Her brain anchored
to the bad side
of the female.

Jealous, she hisses,
wanting, she loves,
rejected, she sulks.

Conceived on a dustbin,
born queen of everything
and knows it.

New Year

The closed circuit of the year
has threaded its electric
through seasons,
bolting bursts
of flowers and death.

And now it is gone.

I raise a drink to myself
and think:

this year, what did I do,
except split myself?
One for me,
and one for you.

I think of our home that contains you.
That which contained me

before I left.

And outside, Aberystwyth's
sharp winter air carries the sound
of a crowd in countdown, the
flood of cheers.

I eye the bottom of my glass,
re-fill it.

Hiraeth

A daisy chain of
verse meshed over Cadair to the Black Mountains
Aneirin, Taliesin, Anonymous...

keeps us all under these skies,
clouded still with the blood of centuries
Marchlew's spears flying, axes falling,
the mead sunk at Catraeth.
We are not defeated,
I live. Cymraes,

clinging to the rocks
of Idris.

New York

New York stole my youth,
and trapped it on a freezing sidewalk.
Forever, that shot –
it doesn't even exist in the camera.
The camera broke.

God, that sweet chestnut
of autumn, the leaves cornflaking
the pavements,
The odd tramp finding a bed.
We stepped over them on the way
back from the Irish bar.
Arguing.

You spent all night on the roof terrace,
I went to bed and pulled the scratchy covers
over the cold, my gratitude on the wane.
But our argument slipped off your skin the next
  morning,
in the shower, as I smoked
my anger out
of the window eyeing
the smooth yellow snake below.

N

Nic is picking flaws
in threads of air,
banging her fist
against the shell of
her life.
The ceiling is slammed shut.

The children just keep coming.

Each formed from the kernel
of men whose
names are just names
and no more.
She is
swimming through pitted
detritus of old thoughts, half-fuzzed
and tobacco stained.

Her life might start any day.

List

1. The grey mist
   and birdsong of
   4am

2. Hang on – where
   did I – it was
   here somewhere

3. I'm sure. Who was he?
   That man, with
   the coat?

4. Nothing is as remote
   as who you were
   yesterday.

5. Simple things:
   I thought I was special.
   I'm not.

6. I haunt myself,
   a bad photo
   taken daily.

7. I wrench through
   marshy earth.
   My life

8. was in here.
   somewhere.

SWF

Scaffolding herself on my bones,
she rakes my ashes, she'd taken my place,
my mirror,
my clothes.

Determined, she admires
herself. The stolen visor
provides what she wants.
A beauty. She is sure.
No! She won't work
the earth for what's beneath.

She stole my mirror,
She stole my mirror.

Forgetting the contours
of what went before,
she moulds
the negative image:
black
becomes
blonde

but the transfer won't work.
It is too fragile to last.

My reflection is behind her,
still here inside the glass.

After the Day

This shining prism
of sandstone hangs on to Pi
and density.
It is untrodden by all
but an ant. He scales the dusty walls
for nothing. He is bored.
The light slides up the
triangular walls, marking time
to an emptied city.

*

Beyond oak, intricate
carvings lead to pages
of a book, turned by the breeze,
in a previously
sealed room. This precious
book is littered with the script
celebrated once,
for some reason.

*

And a room of missiles
remain untouched behind
shatterproof solid steel.
A rhythmic green light flashes –
pulsar of forgotten codes.
No key will unlock doors
trained to an iris.

There is nobody here,
nobody.

Cader

The morning to the brinked insomniac.
The glass air's freshness too fresh.
She stands in the shadow of Idris,
Thumb out, bags packed.

Early spring, 6am.
Her eyes splinter under iced
light, thinks of the bottle he drank
last night.

Strange morning. Eyes dry.
She has to go. Ten cars pass and she'll
go back in, ok twenty, thirty.
One pulls up. She gets in

and is gone.

Shouldering

This morning has

loosened you
like a milk tooth.

And what can the milk tooth do?

I thought that
you had it –
not that it had you.
But it was toying,
blowing your youth away,
like a season's worth.
You were the first to come visit
the life we had made together.
You found us and
sat and drank tea.

Now it's summing you up,
sizing you down.

You lost the sight
in one eye
on Thursday night.
Today you say goodbye
to your sons.

Spring 2004

We grew with the
summer that year.

Today the thin spite
of the Aberystwyth air, some six
years in the future
released me back
to the yellowed attic drawer of
our past.

I couldn't ever imagine, back then
that the bath
you watched me in,
could ever dissolve
into hints and nudges,
sharp stabs at buried senses.
Couldn't imagine the smoke air
we lived in would get banned
and burned up in the hurt
of divorce.

Remember how we waxed
with the trees
pushing
life forwards?
The night was built
for love, the days
for nothing but love.
We grew with the summer
that year, but when
the light grew dim,
we let it.

Viktor's Trap

If you can imagine a world
emptied
of sound, the softscape
of falling snow and
ceaseless mourn-
drift
erasing all but the
shape
of a forest.

Some white-furred god
put his finger on time
here, sent all but the bloodiest
to sleep.
His unbound breath collects
in pockets of thickened white,
dissolving, moving, airlifted
and silent. Adds a
foot to each fir hand
Until the only sound –
the towelled ice fall,
powdery impact, a branch hinge swinging
and nothing.

And then.
A man.

He carries spring-
shouldered metal,
a wolf-mouthed gape, waiting.

The gift
is placed, is one with the white cot
of winter.

It stares upwards, blank and ready.

*

His hands are leather packed
flame-saucers, setting
a self-assured path
through trees. Invisibility
not required by one
whose jaw-cutting claws
and yellow-inch teeth
make a friend of everything.

He ambles his borough,
sends snow flying skywards
under his ten feet
of density
and steps

onto the one square foot
of forest,
that holds fangs
to match his own.

The bone clamp sends the
viper's kiss boring through
his blackened lips
stripping trees in full tremble
of their wares.

He is a burst cable, dancing
fire-footed, roaring at the
pulse of caustic nerves,

sinking, crying, rocks
clumsied on his edge
that can't take the weight.
Rejecting himself, his mother's
son now.

The forest sold him.

He colours the world red,
his oak chested shout
thinning.
The forest watches,

night falls, it falls.

The Morning, Advancing

I settled like a baby
on the knees of dawn.
The new day throwing out
dilations of purple and
prussic strips of clouds,
buzzards screeched
above.

I fell back asleep, boring through
full air
drilling weight
away, and time.

Outside, the thick sleeved stars
retreated,
the boxed up sun
shut up till now,
expanded.

Clairvoyant

Guardian,
I see your shape brewing
against the autumn leaves
fleshing out
and falling
cloudily
into being.

You threaten in mirrors and
in trees, the fullness of you
faceless.

We have known each other a long time now.

My shaman friend, you man-shaped thing
of the forest.

I see you, I see you.

Coal

The coal was thick money
squatting under mountains,
tightening in knotted
walls and racing through
dwarf-earth under
the feet of reasonable men.

Oh, the science
of spooning it out!
Dragon black,
extracted, sleight-of-hand,
the tablecloth at quickspeed,
crockery still standing,
earth still standing.
Conjurer, miner,
the physics.

Manoeuvres

42% of the American public believe that Saddam Hussein was responsible for 9/11[1]

Najem sits in the dirt.
His grief too new to find voice. It is growing
against the force of his fear
that when it happens
it will kill him.
His wife is a wailing dam.
Earlier, Nadia tapped at the showerhead,
Threw a joke at her sister before the

wait

for water was culled
by the window smashing burst
of collapsing house dust.

The missile lodged in her chest, the missile gifted
in coloured scrawl
'For Saddam'.

[1]Arundhati Roy, *The Guardian*, April 2nd 2003

Letter to Judges Altham and Bromley from Elizabeth Devise's Familiar

I escaped gaol, and the noose,
the fat-handed peasant grip
of the ignorant.
I slipped out of space instead,
fell to the dimension
that bore me,
avoiding their eyes, their pitiful restraints.

She was taken, yes...

I screamed blue murder to the night's ear,
howled raw the half of me that
existed without
Elizabeth.

We shared a soul, filled it
with murders and schemes sculpted in clay,
married
in blood, pins,
feathers.

Fireside we built a life, spun spells from stars and
salted pentagrams
that smoked the mists of spirits
condemned. Remember,

I am the half that doesn't die.

The forest might just fling me forward,
have me stalk your footsteps,
should I choose it.

I'll trickle upwards in silver flame,
grow a shape amongst
the autumn-broken leaves.

I'll stand, four legged,
wolf coated, sharp of tooth
and talking

the language of death
the language of Him.

Cabal

Me? You thought me something
once.

On your arm we were
centripetal, a gold-
wash of angles, absorbent
as any galaxy
through a champagne flute.
Oh! How the world fell
to us in orbit;
how they gathered in their velvet and
crepe, their teal-eyed
feathers
drinking us.
My *billet*? My
inventory of blue
eyes, a pearl
décolletage and you,
you felt me your pet
love

for the night, as you
crushed the colour
of me into oak panelled walls.
That night as men
lounged wide-legged
and rum sunken,
as a horse-high giggle struck the air and rose
as distant cutlery clanked in kitchen quarters under
fat stropped hands as

the music fingered
grooves in statesmen
hunched drunk and dancing, eyes closed.
The falling ribbons of opium smoke.

We ran through rooms
each its own chapter, a different story.
You chased me to the gardens,
the fountains upon us,
the sharp sober of
a viscous stone bed, water weeds threatening
my balance, my kohl
melting in the dark. The sudden heaviness
of silk.

Our rented moon blessed us
and only us, her ambassador
children, her poet darlings.

They hadn't invented the music
to match us then.
Our challenge too anarchic
to contain in the iambic strings
that bent the soft June morning
that opened to us
two Piscean halves,

               completing.

The unwed scandal of us!
A lunar consecration
of bodies aligned. Drying

in the morning sun
as we slept.

On waking, we exchanged green blades
for rings. Later, my coach removed me, dropped me in
  a place

you never visited.

This year, somebody else dents
your grassbound haunt.
                    Somebody else
plays the nymph,

but I was something to you.

once.

Acknowledgements

Some of these poems, or earlier versions of them, have appeared in *NAP Magazine, Twiyo Magazine, The Poetry of Yoga* and *Cheval* (volumes 4 and 5). 'Amelia', 'Winter for the Robin' and 'Nigeria' collectively won *The Terry Hetherington Young Writers Award 2011*.

Many thanks to the best editor a writer could wish to work with, Kathryn Gray.

Finally, I am grateful for the support of my friends and family, to Ed (and the tribe) and to Steph. Thank you also to Ian for being a patron of sorts. My gratitude also to Richard, Claire and Eluned. Lastly, to Aida, Jean and Alan: thank you for your continued support.

Other Harbours
Anna Lewis

PARTHIAN

You, Me and the Birds
Alan Kellermann

Stalking Paloma
Ifor Thomas

www.parthianbooks.com